Jack Russell terrier

This lively, clever little dog has lots of energy – you might see it bounding along, wagging its tail.

Farm cat

Watch for cats prowling around the farm hunting rats and mice, or sleeping in a sunny spot.

Hens have shorter tails than cockerels

Plymouth Rock chicken

This chicken has black-and-white stripes – known as 'bars' – on its feathers, and a yellow beak and legs.

In the barn

Bronze turkey
This big turkey gets its name from the coppery sheen on its dark brown feathers.

Hens lay brown eggs

Buff Orpington chicken
A plump chicken with dense, light brown feathers. Spot its pale pink beak and legs, and its red comb.

Clydesdale horse
You might see this heavy horse pulling a cart or doing other farm work, although these days farmers often use tractors instead.

Has long, silky hair around its hooves

Saanen goat

A large goat that gives lots of milk. It needs shelter on hot days to stop its white skin getting sunburned.

Angora rabbit

Notice this fluffy rabbit's thick fur – it can be spun into yarn to make clothing, just like a sheep's wool.

Eggs are pinkish-white

Light Sussex chicken

Look carefully at the black feathers around its neck – each one has a delicate white edge. It has black tail feathers, too.

In the fields

Holstein Friesian cow
One of the most popular kinds of dairy cow because it gives so much milk. Its patchy coat makes it easy to identify.

Shire horse
Similar to a Clydesdale (page 4) but even bigger and stronger. Spot the long hair (known as 'feathers') around its hooves.

Suffolk sheep
Common all around the world, this sheep has a short, dense, creamy fleece and a velvety black face and legs.

Hereford cow

A rusty-brown cow with a white face and underbelly. It's tough enough to live in hot or cold climates.

Texel sheep

This stocky, muscular sheep has no wool on its head or legs. Notice its short, wide face and grey nose.

Look for its curved horns

Alpine goat

You might see this curious, mischievous goat jumping up on hay bales or logs to see what's going on.

Ponds and pastures

Aylesbury duck
You'll see all kinds of ducks paddling on ponds, or waddling about on land looking for food. This one has a pinkish beak.

Cayuga duck
This duck's dark, glossy feathers shimmer green in the sunlight. Its eggs are sometimes black or grey.

Khaki Campbell duck
Gets its name from the khaki (greenish-brown) colour of its feathers. This is a male – females are light brown all over.

Eggs are large and creamy-white

Nubian goat
This tall goat is easy to recognize thanks to its long ears, which hang down next to its face instead of sticking up.

Donkey
Although a donkey can carry heavy loads, it's often just kept as a companion for horses or ponies. Listen for its braying call.

Look for its big, pointed ears

Large White pig
In summer, you might spot one rolling in mud to stop its pale pink skin getting sunburned.

Hills and dales

Border Collie
A very intelligent, speedy and energetic dog. You might see one or more working with a farmer to round up sheep.

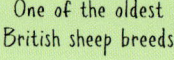

Cotswold sheep
Look for its long, curled locks of thick fleece, which often hang in a fringe over its forehead.

One of the oldest British sheep breeds

Badger Face Welsh Mountain sheep
This hardy sheep can live on all kinds of rough, hilly land. It gets its name from the black stripes on its head.

Patches can be black or brown

Jacob sheep

A white sheep with patchy markings. Count its horns – most of them have four, but some have just two, or six!

Belted Galloway cow

This cow never has horns. Spot the white stripe or 'belt' that goes all the way around its body, under its belly.

Highland cow

Easy to recognize thanks to its long, wide-set horns and shaggy coat, which protects it in wet and windy weather.

Moorland

Swaledale sheep
Common in hilly places in the north of England. Look for the white patches around its eyes and nose, and its curled horns.

Dartmoor pony
If you visit Dartmoor in the UK, keep a lookout for these hardy ponies roaming free. They're also kept for riding.

Ponies may have lived on Dartmoor for 3000 years

Red deer
You might see this deer living wild or on a farm. Only males (stags) have antlers, which fall off each winter and regrow in spring.

Herdwick sheep

Lives high in the hills in the Lake District, England. Its coarse grey wool protects it from the cold and rain.

Aberdeen Angus cow

This Scottish cow is usually black, but you'll sometimes spot a reddish-brown one too. It's very popular in America.

Usually hornless

Comes from the west of Scotland

Hebridean sheep

A small black or dark brown sheep. Spot its curved horns – it may have more than two.

Coasts and islands

Manx Loaghtan sheep
Originally from the Isle of Man. Notice its 'mouse-brown' fleece – that's what its name means in the Manx language.

Jersey cow
This cow came from Jersey in the Channel Islands, but it's now very popular all around the world because of its creamy milk.

Small, and usually light golden-brown

Golden Guernsey goat
Gets its name from its silky coat, which can be any shade between dark gold and pale blonde, and the island it comes from.

Shetland sheepdog
This clever, reliable little dog comes from the Shetland Isles in Scotland, where it was bred to herd the small island sheep.

Orkney sheep
Unlike most mammals, it can live almost entirely on seaweed, which it finds on the beaches of Orkney, Scotland.

Only about the height of a medium-sized dog

Shetland pony
Small but strong. Once kept for farm work on the Shetland Isles, today you're more likely to see children riding them.

Rare breeds

White Park cow
This ancient breed has lived in Britain for over 2,000 years. Spot the dark tips at the ends of its wide, curved horns.

Tamworth pig
Easy to recognize thanks to its bright red-gold coat and big, pricked-up ears.

Closely related to wild boars

Bagot goat
Small, with shaggy fur and long horns. You might see them grazing on country estates or nature reserves.

Suffolk Punch horse

A powerful working horse, once used for ploughing fields. Its smooth coat is always chestnut-coloured.

Oxford Sandy and Black pig

Gingery-brown, with black patches. Look for its large ears flopping down over its eyes.

Sometimes known as the Oxford Forest pig

Bourbon Red turkey

First bred over 100 years ago in Kentucky, America, this big turkey has glossy, mahogany-brown feathers.

Unusual animals

Alpaca
Originally from Peru, alpacas are now farmed around the world for their soft, water-repellent fleece.

Quail
Watch for this little bird scurrying along the ground. Its tiny eggs are only a third the size of a chicken's.

Mangalitza pig
The only kind of pig with a thick, curly coat. You might see them snuffling around, hunting for fallen acorns.

Coat grows thicker and longer in winter

Sometimes kept to guard sheep or goats

Llama
Looks a bit like an alpaca, but bigger. Count its toes – it has two on each foot, just like its other relative, the camel.

Ostrich
This long-legged bird lays the biggest eggs of any land animal. It's also kept for its decorative feathers.

Look for its long, curved horns

Water buffalo
In Europe, it's often kept for its milk, which is used to make soft cheese such as mozzarella.

Farm wildlife

Lapwing
Huge flocks of these black and white birds might be seen on ploughed fields in winter. Spot their long head crests.

Usually seen between October and April

Fieldfare
A winter visitor to the UK. Keep a lookout for flocks of them perching in hedgerows, eating berries.

Harvest mouse
This tiny mouse is only as long as your finger! It can use its tail to grip and swing as it climbs tall stems of grass or crops.

Barn owl

Swoops silently over farmland at night hunting small animals, often roosting in barns during the day.

Honey bee

You'll see these bees buzzing around flowers from April to October, collecting pollen and nectar to make food and honey.

50,000 or more might live together

Brown hare

You're most likely to spot one in a field at dawn or dusk, especially in springtime. Notice its big, black-tipped ears.

Spotting chart

Once you've spotted an animal from this book, find its sticker at the back, and stick it on this chart in the space below its name.

Aberdeen Angus cow	Alpaca	Alpine goat	Angora rabbit	Aylesbury duck
Badger Face Welsh Mountain sheep	Bagot goat	Barn owl	Belted Galloway cow	Border Collie
Bourbon Red turkey	Bronze turkey	Brown hare	Buff Orpington chicken	Cayuga duck
Clydesdale horse	Cotswold sheep	Dartmoor pony	Donkey	Embden goose
Farm cat	Fieldfare	Golden Guernsey goat	Harvest mouse	Hebridean sheep

Herdwick sheep	Hereford cow	Highland cow	Holstein Friesian cow	Honey bee
Jack Russell terrier	Jacob sheep	Jersey cow	Khaki Campbell duck	Lapwing
Large White pig	Light Sussex chicken	Llama	Mangalitza pig	Manx Loaghtan sheep
Nubian goat	Orkney sheep	Ostrich	Oxford Sandy and Black pig	Plymouth Rock chicken
Quail	Red deer	Rhode Island Red chicken	Saanen goat	Shetland pony
Shetland sheepdog	Shire horse	Suffolk Punch horse	Suffolk sheep	Swaledale sheep
Tamworth pig	Texel sheep	Water buffalo	White Leghorn chicken	White Park cow

Index

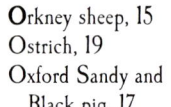

Aberdeen Angus cow, 13
Alpaca, 18
Alpine goat, 7
Angora rabbit, 5
Aylesbury duck, 8

Badger Face Welsh
    Mountain sheep, 10
Bagot goat, 16
Barn owl, 21
Belted Galloway cow, 11
Border Collie, 10
Bourbon Red turkey, 17
Bronze turkey, 4
Brown hare, 21
Buff Orpington chicken, 4

Cayuga duck, 8
Clydesdale horse, 4
Cotswold sheep, 10

Dartmoor pony, 12
Donkey, 9

Embden goose, 2

Farm cat, 3
Fieldfare, 20

Golden Guernsey goat, 14

Harvest mouse, 20
Hebridean sheep, 13
Herdwick sheep, 13
Hereford cow, 7
Highland cow, 11
Holstein Friesian cow, 6
Honey bee, 21

Jack Russell terrier, 3
Jacob sheep, 11
Jersey cow, 14

Khaki Campbell duck, 8

Lapwing, 20
Large White pig, 9
Light Sussex chicken, 5
Llama, 19

Mangalitza pig, 18
Manx Loaghtan sheep, 14

Nubian goat, 9

Orkney sheep, 15
Ostrich, 19
Oxford Sandy and
    Black pig, 17

Plymouth Rock
    chicken, 3

Quail, 18

Red deer, 12
Rhode Island Red
    chicken, 2

Saanen goat, 5
Shetland pony, 15
Shetland sheepdog, 15
Shire horse, 6
Suffolk Punch horse, 17
Suffolk sheep, 6
Swaledale sheep, 12

Tamworth pig, 16
Texel sheep, 7

Water buffalo, 19
White Leghorn chicken, 2
White Park cow, 16

First published in 2023 by Usborne Publishing Limited, 83–85 Saffron Hill, London EC1N 8RT, United Kingdom. usborne.com
Copyright © 2023 Usborne Publishing Limited. The name Usborne and the Balloon logo are trade marks of Usborne Publishing Limited. All rights reserved. No part of this publication may be reproduced, stored in a retrieval system or transmitted in any form or by any means without the prior permission of the publisher. Printed in China. UKE.